I0840602

NEVER FORGET

Or the story of how to get photographic memory skills

GEORGE MIHALACHE

Copyright © 2018 George Mihalache

All rights reserved.

ISBN: 9781728939339

DEDICATION

This book is inspired by the character known as Sheldon.

(The Big Bang Theory)

CONTENTS

ACKNOWLEDGMENTS

Long long time ago, in a small Eastern European country, when I was 6 or 7, I read my first course on how to read faster. I do not remember the author now, probably was a Russian name (see the irony), but I consider that as the point when I started to train my brain and its skills. Thank you unknown author, wherever you are now!

NEVER FORGET

CHAPTER 1

MEMORY AS
A BLINDING LIGHT

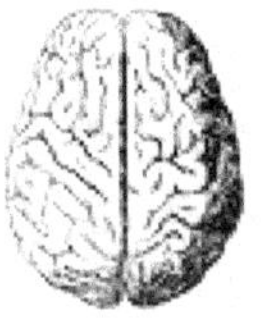

Before we start our learning journey, I will explain few bits and bobs about the brain, the memory and how do they function and coexists together in a close interdependence. Let's define the following terms:

Sensory memory

It is the shortest-term element of memory, defined as the ability to retain impressions of sensory information after the original stimuli have ended. It acts as a buffer for stimuli received via the five senses (sight, hearing, smell, taste and touch), which are retained accurately, but not for long. Think at your ability to look at something and remember what it looked like with just a second of observations. This is sensory memory. If the stimuli detected by our senses are deliberately ignored, they disappear almost instantaneously. If they are perceived, they enter our sensory memory. This will happen without any conscious attention and it is considered to be totally outside of the conscious control. Our brain is designed to only process information data that will be useful at a later date, and it will allow the rest to pass by unnoted. As the information is perceived, it is therefore stored in the sensory memory automatically and unbidden. Unlike the other types of memory, the sensory memory can't be prolonged using rehearsal. The sensory memory is an ultra-short-term memory which decays or degrades very quickly (in the region of 200-500 milliseconds after the perception of an item, less than a second). But the echoic memory is lately thought to last a little longer (perhaps 3-4 seconds). Because of this short time, it is often considered part of perception, but nevertheless represents an essential step for storing information in short term memory. If we refer at the sensory memory related to visual stimuli, we call it iconic memory, for aural stimuli – echoic memory and for touch – haptic memory. The sense of smell is believed to be even more closely linked to memory than the other senses, possible because the olfactory bulb and the olfactory cortex are separated only by 2-3 synapses to the hippocampus and amygdala (parts of the brain involved in the memory process). The smells may be more quickly and strongly associated with memories and their associated emotions than other senses, and memories of a smell may persist for longer, even without constant re-consolidation. In 1960, George Sperling's experiments, using a grid of letters flash for a very short period of time (50 milliseconds), suggest that the upper limit of the sensory memory is approximately 12 items. Information can pass from sensory memory to short term memory via the process of attention (the cognitive process of selectively concentrating on one aspect of the environment ignoring the others), filtering the stimuli to only those which are of interest at any given time.

Short term memory

Short-term memory acts as a kind of "scratch-pad" for temporary recall of the information which is being processed at any point in time, and has been referred to as "the brain's Post-it note". It can be thought of as the ability to remember and process information at the same time. It holds a small amount of information (typically around 7 items or even less) in mind in an active, readily-available state for a short period of time (typically from 10 to 15 seconds, or sometimes up to a minute).

For example, in order to understand this sentence, the beginning of the sentence needs to be held in mind while the rest is read, a task which is carried out by the short-term memory. Other common examples of short-term memory in action are the holding on to a piece of information temporarily in order to complete a task (e.g. "carrying over" a number in a subtraction sum, or remembering a persuasive argument until another person finishes talking), and simultaneous translation (where the interpreter must store information in one language while orally translating it into another). What are actually held in short-term memory, though, are not complete concepts, but rather links or pointers (such as words, for example) which the brain can flesh out from its other accumulated knowledge. However, this information will quickly disappear forever unless we make a conscious effort to retain it, and short-term memory is a necessary step toward the next stage of retention, long-term memory. The transfer of information to long-term memory for more permanent storage can be facilitated or improved by mental repetition of the information or, even more effectively, by giving it a meaning and associating it with other previously acquired knowledge. Motivation is also a consideration, in that information relating to a subject of strong interest to a person is more likely to be retained in long-term memory. According to a recent study at the University of Michigan, the attention and short term memory processing are directly affected by a person's surroundings and environment. Two groups of individuals were tested on attention and working memory performance, one group after a slow walk in a quiet park, another after rushing busy city streets. The second group scored less on the tests. The working memory is used sometimes interchangeably with short term memory, even if technically the working memory is the whole theoretical framework of structures and processes used for temporary storage and manipulation of information, of which the short memory is just one component. The central executive part of the prefrontal cortex at the front of the brain appears to play a fundamental role in short-term and working memory. It both serves as a temporary store for short-term memory, where information is kept available while it is needed for current reasoning processes, but it also "calls up" information from elsewhere in the brain. The central executive controls two neural loops, one for visual data (which activates areas near the visual cortex of the brain and acts as a visual scratch pad), and one for language (the "phonological loop", which uses Broca's area as a kind of "inner voice" that repeats word sounds to keep them in mind). These two scratch pads temporarily hold data until it is erased by the next job. Although the prefrontal cortex is not the only part of the brain involved - it must also cooperate with other parts of the cortex from which it extracts information for brief periods - it is the most important, and Carlyle Jacobsen reported, as early as 1935, that damage to the prefrontal cortex in primates caused short-term memory deficits. The short-term memory has a limited capacity, which can be readily illustrated by the simple expedient of trying to remember a list of random items (without allowing repetition or reinforcement) and seeing when errors begin to creep in. The often-cited experiments by George Miller in 1956 suggest that the number of objects an average human can hold in working memory (known as memory span) is between 5 and 9 (7 $\pm$ 2, which Miller described as the "magical number", and which is sometimes referred to as Miller's Law). However, although this may be approximately true for a population of college students, for example, memory span varies widely with populations tested, and modern estimates are typically lower, of the order of just 4 or 5 items.

As a fun fact, short-term working memory appears to operate phonologically. For instance, whereas English speakers can typically hold seven digits in short-term memory, Chinese speakers can typically remember ten digits. This is because Chinese number words are all single syllables, whereas English are not. The type or characteristics of the information also affects the number of items which can be retained in short-term memory. For instance, more words can be recalled if they are shorter or more commonly used words, or if they are phonologically similar in sound, or if they are taken from a single semantic category (such as sports, for example) rather than from different categories, etc. There is also some evidence that short-term memory capacity and duration is increased if the words or digits are articulated aloud instead of being read sub-vocally (in the head). The relatively small capacity of the short-term memory, compared to the huge capacity of long-term memory, has been attributed by some to the evolutionary survival advantage in paying attention to a relatively small number of important things (e.g. the approach of a dangerous predator, the proximity of a nearby safe haven, etc.) and not to a plethora of other peripheral details which would only interfere with rapid decision-making. "Chunking" of information can lead to an increase in the short-term memory capacity. Chunking is the organization of material into shorter meaningful groups to make them more manageable. For example, a hyphenated phone number, split into groups of 3 or 4 digits, tends to be easier to remember than a single long number. Experiments by Herbert Simon have shown that the ideal size for chunking of letters and numbers, whether meaningful or not, is three. However, meaningful groups may be longer (such as four numbers that make up a date within a longer list of numbers, for example). With chunking, each chunk represents just one of the 5 - 9 items that can be stored in short-term memory, thus extending the total number of items that can be held. The use of mnemonic devices can significantly increase memory, particularly the recall of long lists of names, numbers, etc. One subject was able to increase his digit span (the longest list of number that a person can repeat back in correct order) from 7 to 79 with the use of mnemonic strategies. Akira Haraguchi and Lu Chao's record-breaking recitations of the digits of the number Pi (100,000 and 67,890 digits respectively) also make use of mnemonic systems. It is usually assumed that the short-term memory spontaneously decays over time, typically in the region of 10 - 15 seconds, but items may be retained for up to a minute, depending on the content. However, it can be extended by repetition or rehearsal (either by reading items out loud, or by mental simulation), so that the information re-enters the short-term store and is retained for a further period. When several elements (such as digits, words or pictures) are held in short-term memory simultaneously, they effectively compete with each other for recall. New content, therefore, gradually pushes out older content (known as displacement), unless the older content is actively protected against interference by rehearsal or by directing attention to it. Any outside interference tends to cause disturbances in short-term memory retention, and for this reason people often feel a distinct desire to complete the tasks held in short-term memory as soon as possible. The forgetting of short-term memories involves a different process to the forgetting of long-term memories. When something in short-term memory is forgotten, it means that a nerve impulse has merely ceased being transmitted through a particular neural network. In general, unless an impulse is reactivated, it stops flowing through a network after just a few seconds. Typically, information is transferred from the short-term or working memory to the long-term memory within just a few seconds, although the exact mechanisms, by which this transfer takes place, and whether all or only some memories are retained permanently, remain controversial topics among experts. Richard Schiffrin, in particular, is well known for his work in the 1960 suggesting that ALL memories automatically pass from a short-term to a long-term store after a short time (known as the modal or multi-store or Atkinson-Schiffrin model). However, this is disputed, and it now seems increasingly likely that some kind of vetting or editing procedure takes place. Some researchers (e.g. Eugen Tarnow) have proposed that there is no real distinction between short-term and long-term memory at all, and certainly it is difficult to demarcate a clear boundary between them. However, the evidence of patients with some kinds of anterograde amnesia, and experiments on the way distraction affect the short-term recall of lists, suggest that there are in fact two more or less separate systems.

Long term memory

Long-term memory is, obviously enough, intended for storage of information over a long period of time. Despite our everyday impressions of forgetting, it seems likely that long-term memory actually decays very little over time, and can store a seemingly unlimited amount of information almost indefinitely. Indeed, there is some debate as to whether we actually ever "forget" anything at all, or whether it just becomes increasingly difficult to access or retrieve certain items from memory. Short-term memories can become long-term memory through the process of consolidation, involving rehearsal and meaningful association. Unlike short-term memory (which relies mostly on an acoustic, and to a lesser extent a visual, code for storing information), long-term memory encodes information for storage semantically (i.e. based on meaning and association). However, there is also some evidence that long-term memory does also encode to some extent by sound. For example, when we cannot quite remember a word but it is "on the tip of the tongue", this is usually based on the sound of a word, not its meaning. Physiologically, the establishment of long-term memory involves a process of physical changes in the structure of neurons (or nerve cells) in the brain, a process known as long-term potentiation, although there is still much that is not completely understood about the process. At its simplest, whenever something is learned, circuits of neurons in the brain, known as neural networks, are created, altered or strengthened. These neural circuits are composed of a number of neurons that communicate with one another through special junctions called synapses. Through a process involving the creation of new proteins within the body of neurons, and the electrochemical transfer of neurotransmitters across synapse gaps to receptors, the communicative strength of certain circuits of neurons in the brain is reinforced. With repeated use, the efficiency of these synapse connections increases, facilitating the passage of nerve impulses along particular neural circuits, which may involve many connections to the visual cortex, the auditory cortex, the associative regions of the cortex, etc.

As a matter of fact, several studies have shown that both episodic and semantic long-term memories can be better recalled when the same language is used for both encoding and retrieval. For example, bilingual Russian immigrants to the United States can recall more autobiographical details of their early life when the questions and cues are presented in Russian than when they are questioned in English. This process differs both structurally and functionally from the creation of working or short-term memory. Although the short-term memory is supported by transient patterns of neuronal communication in the regions of the frontal, prefrontal and parietal lobes of the brain, long-term memories are maintained by more stable and permanent changes in neural connections widely spread throughout the brain. The hippocampus area of the brain essentially acts as a kind of temporary transit point for long-term memories, and is not itself used to store information. However, it is essential to the consolidation of information from short-term to long-term memory, and is thought to be involved in changing neural connections for a period of three months or more after the initial learning.

Unlike with short-term memory, forgetting occurs in long-term memory when the formerly strengthened synaptic connections among the neurons in a neural network become weakened, or when the activation of a new network is superimposed over an older one, thus causing interference in the older memory. Over the years, several different types of long-term memory have been distinguished, including explicit and implicit memory, declarative and procedural memory (with a further sub-division of declarative memory into episodic and semantic memory) and retrospective and prospective memory. While older people have more difficulty than the young with rote memorization, such as remembering lists of words or numbers, they actually tend to perform better than young people in the recognition and recall of facts and tasks. This is partly because older people, having accumulated more real-life experience and information, have a denser network of linkages and associations in their long-term memory, and partly because they have had time to more efficiently organize their facts and experiences in a more easily accessible hierarchical form. Long-term memory is often divided into two further main types: explicit (or declarative) memory and implicit (or procedural) memory. Declarative memory ("knowing what") is memory of facts and events, and refers to those memories that can be consciously recalled (or "declared"). It is sometimes called explicit memory, since it consists of information that is explicitly stored and retrieved, although it is more properly a subset of explicit memory. Declarative memory can be further sub-divided into episodic memory and semantic memory. Procedural memory ("knowing how") is the unconscious memory of skills and how to do things, particularly the use of objects or movements of the body, such as tying a shoelace, playing a guitar or riding a bike. These memories are typically acquired through repetition and practice, and are composed of automatic sensorimotor behaviours that are so deeply embedded that we are no longer aware of them. Once learned, these "body memories" allow us to carry out ordinary motor actions more or less automatically. Procedural memory is sometimes referred to as implicit memory, because previous experiences aid in the performance of a task without explicit and conscious awareness of these previous experiences, although it is more properly a subset of implicit memory.

Brain-scan studies have shown that London taxi drivers, who spend years memorizing the city's labyrinthine streets, develop physically larger hippocampi, much as a muscle is enlarged by weight-training. These different types of long-term memory are stored in different regions of the brain and undergo quite different processes. Declarative memories are encoded by the hippocampus, entorhinal cortex and perirhinal cortex (all within the medial temporal lobe of the brain), but are consolidated and stored in the temporal cortex and elsewhere. Procedural memories, on the other hand, do not appear to involve the hippocampus at all, and are encoded and stored by the cerebellum, putamen, caudate nucleus and the motor cortex, all of which are involved in motor control. Learned skills such as riding a bike are stored in the putamen; instinctive actions such as grooming are stored in the caudate nucleus; and the cerebellum is involved with timing and coordination of body skills. Thus, without the medial temporal lobe (the structure that includes the hippocampus), a person is still able to form new procedural memories (such as playing the piano, for example), but cannot remember the events during which they happened or were learned. Children under the age of about seven pick up new languages easily without giving it much conscious thought, using procedural (or implicit) memory. Adults, on the other hand, actively learn the rules and vocabulary of a new language using declarative (or explicit) memory. Perhaps the most famous study demonstrating the separation of the declarative and procedural memories is that of a patient known as "H.M.", who had parts of his medial temporal lobe, hippocampus and amygdala removed in 1953 in an attempt to cure his intractable epilepsy. After the surgery, H.M. could still form new procedural memories and short-term memories, but long-lasting declarative memories could no longer be formed. The nature of the exact brain surgery he underwent, and the types of amnesia he experienced, allowed a good understanding of how particular areas of the brain are linked to specific processes in memory formation. In particular, his ability to recall memories from well before his surgery, but his inability to create new long-term memories, suggests that encoding and retrieval of long-term memory information is mediated by distinct systems within the medial temporal lobe, particularly the hippocampus. The fact that he was able to learn hand-eye coordination skills such as mirror drawing, despite having absolutely no memory of having learned or practiced the task before, also suggested the existence different types of long-term memory, which are now known as declarative and procedural memories. There is strong evidence, notably by studying amnesic patients and the effect of priming, to suggest that implicit memory is largely distinct from explicit memory, and operates through a different process in the brain. Studies of the effects of amnesia have shown that it is quite possible to have an intact implicit memory despite a severely impaired explicit memory. We should have a whole chapter about the role of priming in marketing, manipulation and/or happiness, but this is not the place, nor the time to do it. Priming is the effect in which exposure to a stimulus influences response to a subsequent stimulus, so that, for instance, if a person reads a list of words including the word "concert", and is later asked to complete a word starting with "con", there is a higher probability that they will answer "concert" than, say, "contact", "connect", etc. Studies from amnesic patients indicate that priming is controlled by a brain system separate from the medial temporal system that supports explicit memory. Studies have shown that musicians tend to have a better memory than non-musicians, not just for music, but for words and pictures too. Interestingly, they also tend to use different strategies for memorization, being more likely than non-musicians to group words into similar semantic categories, and less likely to verbalize pictures. Declarative memory can be further sub-divided into episodic memory and semantic memory. Episodic memory represents our memory of experiences and specific events in time in a serial form, from which we can reconstruct the actual events that took place at any given point in our lives. It is the memory of autobiographical events (times, places, associated emotions and other contextual knowledge) that can be explicitly stated. Individuals tend to see themselves as actors in these events, and the emotional charge and the entire context surrounding an event is usually part of the memory, not just the bare facts of the event itself. Semantic memory, on the other hand, is a more structured record of facts, meanings, concepts and knowledge about the external world that we have acquired. It refers to general factual knowledge, shared with others and independent of personal experience and of the spatial/temporal context in which it was acquired. Semantic memories may once have had a personal context, but now stand alone as simple knowledge. It therefore includes such things as types of food, capital cities, social customs, functions of objects, vocabulary, understanding of mathematics, etc. Much of semantic memory is abstract and relational and is associated with the meaning of verbal symbols. The semantic memory is generally derived from the episodic memory, in that we learn new facts or concepts from our experiences. Experiments done on rats in 1970 showed that there are over a million "place cells" in a rat's hippocampus, each of which only becomes active when the rat is located in a very specific part of its environment. All together they can form a very precise cognitive map that tells the animal where it is at any given time. The episodic memory is considered to support and underpin semantic memory. A gradual transition from episodic to semantic memory can take place, in which episodic memory reduces its sensitivity and association to particular events, so that the information can be generalized as semantic memory. Both episodic memory and semantic memory require a similar encoding process. However, semantic memory mainly activates the frontal and temporal cortexes, whereas episodic memory activity is concentrated in the hippocampus, at least initially. Once processed in the hippocampus, episodic memories are then consolidated and stored in the neocortex. The memories of the different elements of a particular event are distributed in the various visual, olfactory and auditory areas of the brain, but they are all connected together by the hippocampus to form an episode, rather than remaining a collection of separate memories. For example, memories of people's faces, the taste of the wine, the music that was playing, etc., might all be part of the memory of a particular dinner with friends. By repeatedly reactivating or "playing back" this particular activity pattern in the various regions of the cortex, they become so strongly linked with one another that they no longer need the hippocampus to act as their link, and the memory of the music that was playing that night, for example, can act as an index entry, and may be enough to bring back the entire scene of the dinner party. Recent research into links between memory and handedness suggest that "mixed-handers" (who typically perform some tasks with one hand and some with the other) tend to show better autobiographical memory than "strong-handers" (who perform almost all tasks with either one hand or the other). It is hypothesized that mixed-handers may have more, or better, communication between the brain's hemispheres than strong-handers, and possibly even a thicker corpus callosum. Our spatial memory in particular appears to be much more confined to the hippocampus, particularly the right hippocampus, which seems to be able to create a mental map of space, thanks to certain cells called "place cells". Episodic memory does also trigger activity in the temporal lobe, but mainly in order to ensure that these personal memories are not mistaken for real life. This difference in the neurological processing of episodic and semantic memory is illustrated by cases of anterograde amnesia cases (a good example being a case in which episodic memory was almost completely lost while semantic memory is retained). A further category of declarative memory, referred to as autobiographical memory, is sometimes distinguished, although really it is just one area of episodic memory. Autobiographical memory refers to a memory system consisting of episodes recollected from an individual's own life, often based on a combination of episodic memory (personal experiences and specific objects, people and events experienced at particular times and places) and semantic memory (general knowledge and facts about the world).

One specific type of autobiographical memory is known as a "flashbulb memory", a highly detailed, exceptionally vivid "snapshot" of a moment or circumstances in which surprising and consequential (or emotionally arousing) news was heard, famous examples being the assassination of John Kennedy, the terrorist bombings on 9/11, etc. Such memories are believed by some to be highly resistant to forgetting, possibly due to the strong emotions that are typically associated with them. However, a number of studies also suggest that flashbulb memories are actually not especially accurate, despite apparently being experienced with great vividness and confidence. Females consistently perform better than males on episodic long-term memory tasks, especially those involving delayed recall and recognition. However, males and females do not differ significantly on working memory and semantic memory tasks. There is also evidence for a negative recall bias in women, which means that females in general are more likely than males to recall their mistakes. An important alternative classification of long-term memory used by some researchers is based on the temporal direction of the memories. Retrospective memory is where the content to be remembered (people, words, events, etc.) is in the past, i.e. the recollection of past episodes. It includes semantic, episodic, autobiographical memory and declarative memory in general, although it can be either explicit or implicit. Prospective memory is where the content is to be remembered in the future, and may be defined as "remembering to remember" or remembering to perform an intended action. It may be either event-based or time-based, often triggered by a cue, such as going to the doctor (action) at 5 p.m. (cue), or remembering to post a letter (action) after seeing a mailbox (cue). Clearly, though, retrospective and prospective memories are not entirely independent entities, and certain aspects of retrospective memory are usually required for prospective memory. Thus, there have been case studies where an impaired retrospective memory has caused a definite impact on prospective memory. However, there have also been studies where patients with an impaired prospective memory had an intact retrospective memory, suggesting that to some extent the two types of memory involve separate processes. MRI studies have shown that the same parts of the brain are used when remembering the past as when imagining a similar event in the future, which shows that past memories are also accessed and drawn on when projections are made into the future. This is sometimes referred to as "mental time travel" as it allows us to project ourselves at will either backwards or forwards in time within our personal lives.

Memory as an overall process

We have already looked at the different stages of memory formation (from perception to sensory memory to short-term memory to long-term memory) in the section on Types of Memory. This section, however, looks at the overall processes involved. Memory is the ability to encode, store and recall information. The three main processes involved in human memory are therefore encoding, storage and recall (retrieval). Additionally, the process of memory consolidation (which can be considered to be either part of the encoding process or the storage process) is treated here as a separate process in its own right. Some of the physiology and neurology involved in these processes is highly complex and technical (and some of it still not completely understood), and lies largely outside the remit of this entry level guide, although at least a general introduction is given here.

Let's talk a bit about perception and encoding. After the initial perception of the stimuli, our brain starts to encode the information. Encoding is the crucial first step into creating a new memory, allowing to the perceived item of interest (the stimulus) to be converted into a construct that can be stored within the brain, and recalled at a later stage from short-term or long-term memory. Encoding is a biological event, starting with perception using our senses. The laying down of a memory starts with the attention (regulated by the frontal lobe and the thalamus), when a memorable event causes neurons to fire more frequently, intensifying the experience and increasing the likelihood of the event to be encoded as a memory. Emotions are closely linked to our attention, and the emotional element of a perceived event is processed using an unconscious pathway in the brain leading to the amygdala. Only after this step is completed, the actual sensations derived from an event are processed. The sensations we just perceive are decoded first in the various sensory areas of the cortex, after that they are combined in the hippocampus to create one single experience. The responsibility for analyzing those inputs and ultimately deciding if they will be allocated to long term memory belongs to the hippocampus. It can be a kind of sorting center where all the new sensations are compared and associated with the previously recorded ones. The various threads of informations are then stored in various different parts of the brain, although we do not know yet the exact way in which these parts are identified and recalled later. The main role played by the hippocampus in memory encoding is been underlined by researching examples of individuals who have had they hippocampus removed or damages, as they cannot create new memory (check about the Anterograde Amnesia). The hippocampus is also one of the few areas of the brain where completely new neurons can grow. The exact mechanism is not completely understood, but memory encoding occurs on different levels, starting with the formation of short-term memory, followed by the conversion to a long term memory via the process of consolidation. The first step is the creation of a memory trace (engram) in response to the external stimuli. An engram is a hypothetical biochemical or biophysical change in the brain's neurons, and we call it hypothetical because no one has ever actually seen or proven the existence of such a construct. The hippocampus, deep within the medial temporal lobe of the brain, will receive connections from the primary sensory areas of the cortex, as well as from the rhinal and entorhinal cortexes and from associative areas. While there anterograde connections converge at the hippocampus, other retrograde pathways emerge from it, returning to primary cortexes. A neural network of cortical synapses effectively records the different associations which are linked to the individual memory.

There are three or four main types of encoding, depending on the classification used to count them:

Acoustic encoding is the processing and encoding of the sound, words or other auditory input for us to store and retrieve later. This is aided by the concept of the phonological loop, allowing input within our echoic memory to be sub-vocally rehearsed in order to facilitate remembering.

Visual encoding is the process of encoding images and visual sensory information. The visual sensory information is temporarily stored within the iconic memory before being encoded into long-term storage. The amygdala (within the medial temporal lobe of the brain which has a primary role in the processing of emotional reactions) fulfills an important role in visual encoding, as it accepts visual input in addition to input from other systems and encodes the positive or negative values of conditioned stimuli. Fun fact – when we are presented with a visual stimulus, the part of the brain which is activated the most depends on the nature of the image. A blurred image activates the visual cortex at the back of the brain. An image of a face that is unknown to us activates the associative and frontal region and a face that is familiar to us will activate the frontal regions, while the visual areas are almost not stimulated at all.

Tactile encoding is the encoding of how something feels, normally through the sense of touch. Physiologically, neurons in the primary somatosensory cortex of the brain react to vibrotactile stimuli caused by the feel of an object.

Semantic encoding is the process of encoding sensory input that has particular meaning or can be applied to a particular context, rather than deriving from a particular sense.

Hint! It is believed that, in general, encoding for short-term memory storage in the brain relies primarily on acoustic encoding, while encoding for long-term storage is more reliant (although not exclusively) on semantic encoding. In a positive example of disfluency (the subjective feeling of difficulty associated with any mental task), a recent study at Princeton University has shown that students learning new material printed in a difficult-to-read font or typeface were able to recall significantly more than those learning the same material in a font considered easy to read. It is believed that presenting information in a way that is hard to digest means that a person has to concentrate more, leading to deeper processing and therefore better retrieval afterwards. Human memory is fundamentally associative, meaning that a new piece of information is remembered better if it can be associated with previously acquired knowledge that is already firmly anchored in memory. The more personally and meaningful the association, the more effective the encoding and consolidation. Elaborate processing that emphasizes meaning and associations that are familiar tends to leads to improved recall. On the other hand, information that a person finds difficult to understand cannot be readily associated with already acquired knowledge, and so will usually be poorly remembered, and may even be remembered in a distorted form due to the effort to comprehend its meaning and associations. For example, given a list of words like "thread", "sewing", "haystack", "sharp", "point", "syringe", "pin", "pierce", "injection" and "knitting", people often also (incorrectly) remember the word "needle" through a process of association.

Because of the associative nature of memory, encoding can be improved by a strategy of organization of memory called elaboration, in which new pieces of information are associated with other information already recorded in long-term memory, thus incorporating them into a broader, coherent narrative which is already familiar. An example of this kind of elaboration is the use of mnemonics, which are verbal, visual or auditory associations with other, easy-to-remember constructs, which can then be related back to the data that is to be remembered. Rhymes, acronyms, acrostics and codes can all be used in this way. Common examples are "Roy G. Biv" to remember the order of the colours of the rainbow, or "Every Good Boy Deserves Flavour" for the musical notes on the lines of the treble clef, which most people find easier to remember than the original list of colours or letters. When we use mnemonic devices, we are effectively passing facts through the hippocampus several times, so that it can keep strengthening the associations, and therefore improve the likelihood of subsequent memory recall.

It has been shown that using two separate study sessions, with time between the sessions, can result in twice the learning as a single study session of the same total time length. This is known as spaced learning (the opposite of cramming), and is designed to avoid the situation where the synapses become "maxed out" or lose their ability to learn new information (also known as the long-term depression or weakening of a synapse connection).

In the same way, associating words with images is another commonly used mnemonic device, providing two alternative methods of remembering, and creating additional associations in the mind. Taking this to a higher level, another method of improving memory encoding and consolidation is the use of a so-called memory palace (also known as the method of loci), a mnemonic techniques that relies on memorized spatial relationships to establish, order and recollect other memories. The method is to assign objects or facts to different rooms in an imaginary house or palace, so that recall of the facts can be activated by mentally "walking though" the palace until it is found. Many top memorizers today use the memory palace method to a greater or lesser degree. Similar techniques involve placing the items at different landmarks on a favorite hike or trip (known as the journey method), or weaving them into a story. But about all these methods we will talk in the next chapters.

The old and popular notion of the brain as a kind of "muscle" which strengthens with repeated use (also known as faculty theory) is now largely discredited. Research, dating back to William James towards the end of the 19th Century, shows that long hours spent memorizing does not build up the powers of memory at all, and, on the contrary, may even diminish it. This is not to say that individual memories cannot be strengthened by repetition, but that, as James found, daily training in the memorization of a poetry of one author, for example, does not improves a person's ability to learn the poetry of another author, or poetry in general.

Many studies have shown that the most vivid

autobiographical memories tend to be of emotional events, which are likely to be recalled more often and with more clarity and detail than neutral events. One theory suggests that high levels of emotional arousal lead to attention narrowing, where the range of sensitive cues from the stimulus and its environment is decreased, so that information central to the source of the emotional arousal is strongly encoded while peripheral details are not (e.g. the so-called "weapon focus effect", in which witnesses to a crime tend to remember the gun or knife in great detail, but not other more peripheral details such as the perpetrator's clothing or vehicle).

Studies suggest that characteristics of the environment are encoded as part of the memory trace, and can be used to enhance retrieval of the other information in the trace. In other words, you can recall more when the environments are similar in both the learning (encoding) and recall phases. Thus, deep-sea divers tend to remember their training more effectively when trained underwater rather than on land, and students perform better on exams by studying in silence, because exams are usually done in silence.

Consolidation is the processes of stabilizing a memory trace after the initial acquisition. It may perhaps be thought of part of the process of encoding or of storage, or it may be considered as a memory process in its own right. It is usually considered to consist of two specific processes, synaptic consolidation (which occurs within the first few hours after learning or encoding) and system consolidation (where hippocampus-dependent memories become independent of the hippocampus over a period of weeks to years). Neurologically, the process of consolidation utilizes a phenomenon called long-term potentiation, which allows a synapse to increase in strength as increasing numbers of signals are transmitted between the two neurons. Potentiation is the process by which synchronous firing of neurons makes those neurons more inclined to fire together in the future. Long-term potentiation occurs when the same group of neurons fire together so often that they become permanently sensitized to each other. As new experiences accumulate, the brain creates more and more connections and pathways, and may "re-wire" itself by re-routing connections and re-arranging its organization. As such a neuronal pathway, or neural network, is traversed over and over again, an enduring pattern is engraved and neural messages are more likely to flow along such familiar paths of least resistance. This process is achieved by the production of new proteins to rebuild the synapses in the new shape, without which the memory remains fragile and easily eroded with time. For example, if a piece of music is played over and over, the repeated firing of certain synapses in a certain order in your brain makes it easier to repeat this firing later on, with the result that the musician becomes better at playing the music, and can play it faster, with fewer mistakes. In this way, the brain organizes and reorganizes itself in response to experiences, creating new memories prompted by experience, education or training. The ability of the connection, or synapse, between two neurons to change in strength, and for lasting changes to occur in the efficiency of synaptic transmission, is known as synaptic plasticity or neural plasticity, and it is one of the important neurochemical foundations of memory and learning.

Reading out loud (or even whispering or mouthing it) forms auditory links in our memory pathways, as well as visual ones from looking at a page or screen. So, we remember ourselves producing and saying the information as well as reading it visually, which may improve our overall retrieval of memories. But this process works best, when just some of the information (e.g. the most important words or concepts) is read out loud, and the rest not, as this takes advantage of the "oddball effect" whereby we remember the more unusual or distinctive information best. It should be remembered that each neuron makes thousands of connections with other neurons, and memories and neural connections are mutually interconnected in extremely complex ways. Unlike the functioning of a computer, each memory is embedded in many connections, and each connection is involved in several memories. Thus, multiple memories may be encoded within a single neural network, by different patterns of synaptic connections. Conversely, a single memory may involve simultaneously activating several different groups of neurons in completely different parts of the brain.

The inverse of long-term potentiation, known as long-term depression, can also take place, whereby the neural networks involved in erroneous movements are inhibited by the silencing of their synaptic connections. This can occur in the cerebellum, which is located towards the back of the brain, in order to correct our motor procedures when learning how to perform a task (procedural memory), but also in the synapses of the cortex, the hippocampus, the striatum and other memory-related structures. Contrary to long-term potentiation, which is triggered by high-frequency stimulation of the synapses, long-term depression is produced by nerve impulses reaching the synapses at very low frequencies, leading them to undergo the reverse transformation from long-term potentiation, and, instead of becoming more efficient, the synaptic connections are weakened. It is still not clear whether long-term depression contributes directly to the storage of memories in some way, or whether it simply makes us forget the traces of some things learned long ago so that new things can be learned.

Sleep (particularly slow-wave, or deep, sleep, during the first few hours) is also thought to be important in improving the consolidation of information in memory, and activation patterns in the sleeping brain, which mirror those recorded during the learning of tasks from the previous day, suggest that new memories may be solidified through such reactivation and rehearsal. Studies have shown that information is transferred between the hippocampus and the cerebral cortex during deep sleep, and sleep appears to be essential for the proper consolidation of long-term memories. However, even daytime naps can help improve memory to some extent, and helps with the memorization of important facts. Memory re-consolidation is the process of previously consolidated memories being recalled and then actively consolidated all over again, in order to maintain, strengthen and modify memories that are already stored in the long-term memory. Several retrievals of memory (either naturally through reflection, or through deliberate recall) may be needed for long-term memories to last for many years, depending on the depth of the initial processing. However, these individual retrievals can take place at increasing intervals; in accordance with the principle of spaced repetition (this is familiar to us in the way that "cramming" the night before an exam is not as effective as studying at intervals over a much longer span of time). The very act of re-consolidation, though, may change the initial memory. As a particular memory trace is reactivated, the strengths of the neural connections may change, the memory may become associated with new emotional or environmental conditions or subsequently acquired knowledge, expectations rather than actual events may become incorporated into the memory. Research into a cognitive disorder known as Korsakoff's syndrome shows that the retrograde amnesia of sufferers follows a distinct temporal curve, in that the more remote the event in the past, the better it is preserved. This suggests that the more recent memories are not fully consolidated and therefore more vulnerable to loss, indicating that the process of consolidation may continue for much longer than initially thought, perhaps for many years. Studies have shown that we often construct our memories after the fact, and that we are susceptible to suggestions from others that help us fill in the gaps in our memories. This malleability of memory is why, for example, a police officer investigating a crime should not show a picture of a single individual to a victim and ask if the victim recognizes the assailant. If the victim is then presented with a line-up and picks out the individual whose picture the victim had been shown, there is no real way of knowing whether the victim is actually remembering the assailant or just the picture. Storage is the more or less passive process of retaining information in the brain, whether in the sensory memory, the short-term memory or the more permanent long-term memory. Each of these different stages of human memory function as a sort of filter that helps to protect us from the flood of information that confront us on a daily basis, avoiding an overload of information and helping to keep us sane. The more the information is repeated or used, the more likely it is to be retained in long-term memory (which is why, for example, studying helps people to perform better on tests). This process of consolidation, the stabilizing of a memory trace after its initial acquisition, is treated in more detail in a separate section.

Since the early neurological work of Karl Lashley and

Wilder Penfield in the Fifties and Sixties, it has become clear that long-term memories are not stored in just one part of the brain, but are widely distributed throughout the cortex. After consolidation, long-term memories are stored throughout the brain as groups of neurons that are primed to fire together in the same pattern that created the original experience, and each component of a memory is stored in the brain area that initiated it (e.g. groups of neurons in the visual cortex store a sight, neurons in the amygdala store the associated emotion). Indeed, it seems that they may even be encoded redundantly, several times, in various parts of the cortex, so that, if one engram (or memory trace) is wiped out, there are duplicates, or alternative pathways, elsewhere, through which the memory may still be retrieved. Therefore, contrary to the popular notion, memories are not stored in our brains like books on library shelves, but must be actively reconstructed from elements scattered throughout various areas of the brain by the encoding process. Memory storage is therefore an ongoing process of reclassification resulting from continuous changes in our neural pathways, and parallel processing of information in our brains. The indications are that, in the absence of disorders due to trauma or neurological disease, the human brain has the capacity to store almost unlimited amounts of information indefinitely. Forgetting, therefore, is more likely to be result from incorrectly or incompletely encoded memories, and/or problems with the recall/retrieval process. It is a common experience that we may try to remember something one time and fail, but then remember that same item later. The information is therefore clearly still there in storage, but there may have been some kind of a mismatch between retrieval cues and the original encoding of the information. "Lost" memories recalled with the aid of psychotherapy or hypnosis are other examples supporting this idea, although it is difficult to be sure that such memories are real and not implanted by the treatment.

A recent study has shown scientifically what criminal lawyers have known for decades, namely that memory is an adaptive process. Apparently trivial or mundane memories from just before an important or traumatic event appear to be kept for a period in a kind of "just-in-case file", and may be retroactively enhanced in case they are useful in interpreting the event. This retroactive strengthening is not immediate, and can take several hours or days to take effect. Having said that, though, it seems unlikely that, as Richard Schiffrin and others have claimed, all memories are stored somewhere in the brain, and that it is only in the retrieval process that irrelevant details are "fast-forwarded" over or expurgated. It seems more likely that the memories which are stored are in some way edited and sorted, and that some of the more peripheral details are never stored.

Forgetting, then, is perhaps better thought of as the temporary or permanent inability to retrieve a piece of information or a memory that had previously been recorded in the brain. Forgetting typically follows a logarithmic curve, so that information loss is quite rapid at the start, but becomes slower as time goes on. In particular, information that has been learned very well (e.g. names, facts, foreign-language vocabulary), will usually be very resistant to forgetting, especially after the first three years. Unlike amnesia, forgetting is usually regarded as a normal phenomenon involving specific pieces of content, rather than relatively broad categories of memories or even entire segments of memory. Theorists disagree over exactly what becomes of material that is forgotten. Some hold that long-term memories do actually decay and disappear completely over time; others hold that the memory trace remains intact as long as we live, but the bonds or cues that allow us to retrieve the trace become broken, due to changes in the organization of the neural network or new experiences, in the same way as a misplaced book in a library is "lost" even though it still exists somewhere in the library. Fun fact! Research using functional magnetic resonance imaging (fMRI) suggests that verbs and nouns are stored in different ways in the brain. Concrete nouns are stored in areas of the brain used to sense or manipulate the referent objects, leading to a theory of meaning based largely on function. Increasing forgetfulness is a normal part of the ageing process, as the neurons in ageing brains lose their connections and start to die off, and, ultimately the brain shrinks and becomes less effective. The hippocampus, which as we have seen is crucial for memory and learning, is one of the first areas of the brain to deteriorate with age. Recent studies in mice involving infusions of blood from young mice into older mice have shown that the old mice that received young blood showed a significant burst of brain cell growth in the hippocampus region (and vice versa), leading to speculation that young blood might represent the antidote to senile forgetfulness (and other ravages of old age). Similar studies on humans with Alzheimer's disease are currently in progress.

Interestingly, it appears not to be possible to deliberately delete memories at will, which can have negative consequences, for example if we experience traumatic events we would actually prefer to forget. In fact, such memories tend to be imprinted even more strongly than normal due to their emotional content, although recent research involving the use of beta blockers (such as propranolol) suggests that it may be possible to tone down the emotional aspects of such memories, even if the memories themselves cannot be erased. The way this works is that the act of recalling stored memories makes them "malleable" once more, as they were during the initial encoding phase, and their re-storage can then be blocked by drugs which inhibit the proteins that enable the emotional memory to be re-saved.

Genuine eidetic or photographic memory (an "unprocessed" sensory memory of sensory events that is as accurate as if the person were still experiencing the original objects or events) is extremely rare, although not unheard of. Most extraordinary memory skills which make claims of photographic memory, however, result from a combination of innate skills, learned tactics, mnemonic devices and extraordinary knowledge bases, rather than eidetic memory as such. Young children, with their lack of verbal and conceptual systems, are more likely to have real eidetic memories than adults. A classic case from the Seventies was a woman named Elizabeth, who was able to write out poetry in a foreign language (of which she had no prior knowledge) several years after seeing the original text. The recall or retrieval of memory refers to the subsequent re-accessing of events or information from the past, which have been previously encoded and stored in the brain. In common parlance, it is known as remembering. During the recall, the brain "replays" a pattern of neural activity that was originally generated in response to a particular event, echoing the brain's perception of the real event. In fact, there is no real solid distinction between the act of remembering and the act of thinking. These replays are not quite identical to the original, though - otherwise we would not know the difference between the genuine experience and the memory - but are mixed with an awareness of the current situation. One corollary of this is that memories are not frozen in time, and new information and suggestions may become incorporated into old memories over time.

Thus, remembering can be thought of as an act of creative reimagination. Because of the way memories are encoded and stored, memory recall is effectively an on-the-fly reconstruction of elements scattered throughout various areas of our brains. Memories are not stored in our brains like books on library shelves, or even as a collection of self-contained recordings or pictures or video clips, but may be better thought of as a kind of collage or a jigsaw puzzle, involving different elements stored in disparate parts of the brain linked together by associations and neural networks. Memory retrieval therefore requires re-visiting the nerve pathways the brain formed when encoding the memory and the strength of those pathways determines how quickly the memory can be recalled. Recall effectively returns a memory from long-term storage to short-term or working memory, where it can be accessed, in a kind of mirror image of the encoding process. It is then re-stored back in long-term memory, thus re-consolidating and strengthening it. Several studies have shown that both episodic and semantic memories can be better recalled when the same language is used for both encoding and retrieval. For example, bilingual Russian immigrants to the United States can recall more autobiographical details of their early life when the questions and cues are presented in Russian than when they are questioned in English. The efficiency of human memory recall is astounding. Most of what we remember is by direct retrieval, where items of information are linked directly a question or cue, rather than by the kind of sequential scan a computer might use (which would require a systematic search through the entire contents of memory until a match is found). Other memories are retrieved quickly and efficiently by hierarchical inference, where a specific question is linked to a class or subset of information about which certain facts are known. Also, the brain is usually able to determine in advance whether there is any point in searching memory for a particular fact (e.g. it instantly recognizes a question like "What is Socrates' telephone number?" as absurd in that no search could ever produce an answer).

There are two main methods of accessing memory: recognition and recall. Recognition is the association of an event or physical object with one previously experienced or encountered, and involves a process of comparison of information with memory, e.g. recognizing a known face, true/false or multiple choice questions, etc. Recognition is a largely unconscious process, and the brain even has a dedicated face-recognition area, which passes information directly through the limbic areas to generate a sense of familiarity, before linking up with the cortical path, where data about the person's movements and intentions are processed. Recall involves remembering a fact, event or object that is not currently physically present (in the sense of retrieving a representation, mental image or concept), and requires the direct uncovering of information from memory, e.g. remembering the name of a recognized person, fill-in the blank questions. Recognition is usually considered to be "superior" to recall (in the sense of being more effective), in that it requires just a single process rather than two processes. Recognition requires only a simple familiarity decision, whereas a full recall of an item from memory requires a two-stage process (indeed, this is often referred to as the two-stage theory of memory) in which the search and retrieval of candidate items from memory is followed by a familiarity decision where the correct information is chosen from the candidates retrieved. Thus, recall involves actively reconstructing the information and requires the activation of all the neurons involved in the memory in question, whereas recognition only requires a relatively simple decision as to whether one thing among others has been encountered before. Sometimes, however, even if a part of an object initially activates only a part of the neural network concerned, recognition may then suffice to activate the entire network. Color may have an effect on our ability to memorize something. People remember color scenes better than black-and-white ones, although only if naturally (as opposed to falsely) coloured. In particular, warm colours, like red, yellow and orange, may help us to memorize things by increasing our level of attention (our ability to select from information available in the environment). The more attention is focused on outside stimuli, the greater the likelihood of those stimuli being stored in long-term memory.

In the Eighties, Endel Tulving proposed an alternative to the two-stage theory, which he called the theory of encoding specificity. This theory states that the memory utilizes information both from the specific memory trace, as well as from the environment in which it is retrieved. Because of its focus on the retrieval environment or state, encoding specificity takes into account context cues, and it also has some advantages over the two-stage theory as it accounts for the fact that, in practice, recognition is not actually always superior to recall. Typically, recall is better when the environments are similar in both the learning (encoding) and recall phases, suggesting that context cues are important. In the same way, emotional material is remembered more reliably in moods that match the emotional content of these memories (e.g. happy people will remember more happy than sad information, whereas sad people will better remember sad than happy information). According to the levels-of-processing effect theory, another alternative theory of memory suggested by

Fergus Craik and Robert Lockhart, memory recall of stimuli is also a function of the depth of mental processing, which is in turn determined by connections with pre-existing memory, time spent processing the stimulus, cognitive effort and sensory input mode. Thus, shallow processing (such as, typically, that based on sound or writing) leads to a relatively fragile memory trace that is susceptible to rapid decay, whereas deep processing (such as that based on semantics and meanings) results in a more durable memory trace. This theory suggests, then, that memory strength is continuously variable, as opposed to the earlier Atkinson-Shiffrin, or multi-store, memory model, which just involves a sequence of three discrete stages, from sensory to short-term to long-term memory. The evidence suggests that memory retrieval is a more or less automatic process. Thus, although distraction or divided attention at the time of recall tends to slow down the retrieval process to some extent, it typically has little to no effect on the accuracy of retrieved memories. Distraction at the time of encoding, on the other hand, can severely impair subsequent retrieval success. The efficiency of memory recall can be increased to some extent by making inferences from our personal stockpile of world knowledge, and by our use of schema (plural: schemata). A schema is an organized mental structure or framework of pre-conceived ideas about the world and how it works, which we can use to make realistic inferences and assumptions about how to interpret and process information. Thus, our everyday communication consists not just of words and their meanings, but also of what is left out and mutually understood (e.g. if someone says "it is 3 o'clock", our knowledge of the world usually allows us to know automatically whether it is 3 AM or 3 PM). Such schemata are also applied to recalled memories, so that we can often flesh out details of a memory from just a skeleton memory of a central event or object. However, the use of schemata may also lead to memory errors as assumed or expected associated events are added that did not actually occur. Several recent studies in the growing area of neuro-education have shown the value of the "testing effect" (or "retrieval effect"), where quizzes a short time after initial learning significantly improves subsequent retrieval of facts and ideas, as well as overall understanding of topics and the ability to solve related problems. Testing helps protect against "proactive interference" (the familiar feeling of being overwhelmed by too much information), and the studies suggest that a quick test is much more effective than en extra hour of study or re-reading.

There are **three main types of recall**:

1. Free recall is the process in which a person is given a list of items to remember and then is asked to recall them in any order (hence the name "free"). This type of recall often displays evidence of either the primacy effect (when the person recalls items presented at the beginning of the list earlier and more often) or the recency effect (when the person recalls items presented at the end of the list earlier and more often), and also of the contiguity effect (the marked tendency for items from neighboring positions in the list to be recalled successively).

2. Cued recall is the process in which a person is given a list of items to remember and is then tested with the use of cues or guides. When cues are provided to a person, they tend to remember items on the list that they did not originally recall without a cue, and which were thought to be lost to memory. This can also take the form of stimulus-response recall, as when words, pictures and numbers are presented together in a pair, and the resulting associations between the two items cues the recall of the second item in

the pair.

3. Serial recall refers to our ability to recall items or events in the order in which they occurred, whether chronological events in our autobiographical memories, or the order of the different parts of a sentence (or phonemes in a word) in order to make sense of them. Serial recall in long-term memory appears to differ from serial recall in short-term memory, in that a sequence in long-term memory is represented in memory as a whole, rather than as a series of discrete items.

Testing of serial recall by psychologists has yielded several general rules:

-more recent events are more easily remembered in order (especially with auditory stimuli);

-recall decreases as the length of the list or sequence increases;

-there is a tendency to remember the correct items, but in the wrong order;

-where errors are made, there is a tendency to respond with an item that resembles the original item in some way (e.g. "dog" instead of "fog", or perhaps an item physically close to the original item);

-repetition errors do occur, but they are relatively rare;

-if an item is recalled earlier in the list than it should be, the missed item tends to be inserted immediately after it;

-if an item from a previous trial is recalled in a current trial, it is likely to be recalled at its position from the original trial.

If we assume that the "purpose" of human memory is to use past events to guide future actions, then keeping a perfect and complete record of every past event is not necessarily a useful or efficient way of achieving this. So, in most people, some specific memories may be given up or converted into general knowledge (i.e. converted from episodic to semantic memories) as part of the ongoing recall/re-consolidation process, so that that we are able to generalize from experience. It is also possible that false memories (or at least wrongly interpreted memories) may be created during recall, and carried forward thereafter. Research into false memory creation is particularly associated with Elizabeth Loftus' work in the Seventies. Among many other experiments in this area (see the side panel on the Psychogenic Amnesia page, for example), she showed how the precise wording of a question about memories (e.g. "the car hit" or "the car smashed into") can dramatically influence the recall and re-creation of memories, and can even permanently change those memories for future recalls - a phenomenon which is not lost on the legal profession. It is thought that it may even be possible, up to a point, to choose to forget, by blocking out unwanted memories during recall, a process achieved by frontal lobe activity, which inhibits the laying down or re-consolidation of a memory. However, there is a rare condition called hyperthymesia (also known as hypermnesia or superior autobiographical memory) in which a few people show an extraordinary capacity to recall detailed specific events from a person's personal past, without relying on practised mnemonic strategies. Although only a handful of cases of hyperthymesia have ever been definitively confirmed, some of these cases are quite startling, such as a California woman who could recall every day in complete detail from the age of 14 onwards, a young English girl with an IQ of 191 who had a perfect photographic memory spanning almost 18 years, and a Russian man known simply as S. who was only able to forget anything by a deliberate act of will. One of the most famous cases, known as A.J., described it as a burden rather than a gift, but others seem to be able to organize and compartmentalize their prodigious memories and do not appear to feel that their brains are cluttered with excess information.

Memory recall appears to be state-dependent, at least to some extent. Studies have shown that, when material is learned under the influence of a drug or alcohol, for example, it is subsequently recalled much more efficiently when in the same drug state than when sober. Similarly, individuals tend to retrieve information more easily when it has the same emotional content as their current emotional state, and when the emotional state at the time of retrieval is similar to the emotional state at the time of encoding. Age associated memory impairment is a label for the general degradation of memory which results from ageing. It is a natural process, seen in many animals as well as humans, which often begins in our twenties and tends to get noticeably worse as we reach our fifties. While some specific abilities do decline with age, though, overall memory generally remains strong for most people through their seventies. Episodic memory (our memory of experiences and specific events in time) in particular is impaired in normal ageing. On the other hand, in the absence of specific neurological disorders, implicit or procedural memory typically shows little or no decline with age, short-term memory shows only a little decline, and semantic knowledge, such as vocabulary, actually tends to improve somewhat with age. Normal ageing is not responsible for causing memory disorders as such, but it is associated with a general decline in cognitive and neural systems, including memory. As people age, the likelihood of cholinergic dysfunction, beta-amyloid deposits, hippocampal neurofibrillary tangles or neuritic plaques in the cortex of the brain increases, so that memory connections can become blocked, memory functions decrease and the likelihood of memory disorders like dementia and Alzheimer's disease increases. Ageing is the single greatest risk factor for neurodegenerative diseases in general. Recent research has identified a transitional state between the cognitive changes of normal ageing and Alzheimer's disease, known as mild cognitive impairment, where some memory loss occurs, but is not so severe that it interferes with normal daily functioning. More severe memory loss is defined as dementia, of which Alzheimer's is just one common variant. Those who experience mild cognitive impairment are at a significantly higher risk of developing Alzheimer's disease or other types of dementia, especially after events like strokes.

As one successful experiment proves it, a recent report by the Society for Neuroscience suggests that infusions of blood from young mice can reverse the memory decline in older mice, and vice versa. It is not clear just how this effect works. Although the brain does not change its overall structure or grow whole new batches of neurons over time, the connections between them change during the normal process of learning, as synapses are reinforced and neural cells make more and stronger connections with each other. As we begin to age, however, these connections begin to falter and weaken, in the same way as other biological processes deteriorate and become more fragmented over time, and this begins to affect how easily we can retrieve memories. In particular, as the brain ages, the white matter which links together different parts of the brain, begins to die off, largely because the blood flow supplied to the brain is not as healthy as in the young, which causes memory to become impaired. Also, the production of the chemical messengers (neurotransmitters) used to carry signals through the brain is also reduced, perhaps by as much as 50% between young adulthood and old age, which impairs our ability to think and perform memory tasks. The decline theory of forgetting suggests that, essentially, forgetting occurs when the memory is not exercised, or the information in question is not retrieved often enough to re-consolidate memories. This is illustrated by the order in which words tend to be forgotten in old age: proper nouns, which are typically used less often, are usually the first words to go, followed by common nouns, then adjectives, verbs and, lastly, exclamations and interjections.

A 2011 study for the American Journal of Clinical Nutrition suggests that a diet high in fruit and vegetables, particularly fruits that are high in Vitamin C and anti-oxidants, can help protect against memory loss due to ageing. One theory for why this happens, at the cellular level, is that ageing causes major cell loss in a tiny region at the front of the brain that leads to a drop in the production of a neurotransmitter called acetylcholine, which is vital to learning and memory. In addition, the brain itself shrinks in size to some extent, and becomes less efficient as we age. In particular, the hippocampus, which is essential to the proper functioning of the processes of memory, loses about 5% of its nerve cells with each passing decade, up to a total loss of 20% by the age of about 80. There are, however, several other environmental factors which may combine to speed up memory decline, including the inheritance of unhealthy genes, exposure to toxins and poisons, or lifestyle choices like smoking, drinking or bad diet. Physical exercise and mental stimulation can improve mental function in general, and therefore help to slow memory decline, although there is no "magic bullet" solution as some might claim. It is also becoming apparent that some drugs used to treat other age-related diseases and conditions may have a deleterious effect on memory and hasten the onset of dementia, among them: anti-anxiety drugs (e.g. benzodiazepines); cholesterol-lowering drugs (e.g. statins); anti-depressant drugs (e.g. tricyclics); anti-seizure and anti-convulsant drugs; narcotic painkillers and opioids; Parkinson's drugs (e.g. dopamine agonists); hypertension drugs (e.g. beta-blockers); sleeping aids (e.g. non-benzodiapezine sedatives); incontinence drugs (e.g. anti-cholinergics); first generation antihistamines.

Normal human memory powers peak at the age of 25, after which they start to decline. At this time, the brain is capable of remembering over 200 bits of information per second, as well as controlling body movements at the same time, far outstripping the performance of any computer.

Alcohol, and the effects of alcohol on memory and general cognitive functioning, has been the subject of much research over the years. Alcohol acts as a general central nervous system depressant, but it affects some areas of the brain more than others. Specifically, it leads to distraction and inattention and significantly inhibits neuronal activity in the hippocampus, which impairs memory encoding since the hippocampus plays an important role in the formation of new declarative memories. Because procedural memory functions more or less automatically, retrieval of procedural memory ("remembering how") is not as severely impaired by alcohol as retrieval of declarative memory ("remembering what"). Alcohol particularly impairs the encoding of episodic memory (that part of declarative memory that relates to our personal experiences and specific events in time), especially for certain types of recall, such as cued recall, the recognition of completed word fragments and free recall. A "blackout" is an example of a difficulty in the encoding of episodic memories due to high doses of alcohol. It is caused by a rapid increase in blood alcohol concentration, which in turn distorts the activity of neurons in the hippocampus, thus impairing person's ability to form new episodic memories. Alcohol also severely disrupt the encoding and storage process of new semantic memories (our memory of facts, meanings and acquired knowledge about the external world), although apparently not that of previously learned information. Alcohol also impairs short-term (working) memory, although mainly by affecting certain mnemonic strategies and executive processes rather than by shrinking the basic holding capacity of working memory or by physically altering the structure of the those parts of the brain which are critical for working memory function. Although light to moderate drinking does not appear to impair long-term cognitive functioning significantly (and according to some studies, may actually decrease the risk of cognitive decline), heavy drinking and chronic alcoholism is associated with long-term impairment in sustained attention and working memory function, especially visual working memory. Serious over-consumption of alcohol, especially in comparison with the intake of other foods, can cause a thiamine deficiency, leading to a much more serious form of amnesia known as Korsakoff's syndrome. One-time, or light, use of stimulants, such as cocaine, amphetamines or caffeine can improve memory recall in humans. However, heavy or prolonged use of stimulants or marijuana is associated with small but significant impairments in working memory and episodic memory retrieval.

Now is the time to delve into the biology of the brain, in order to use our visual cues for a better understanding. The human brain is hugely interconnected but three major components can be identified: the cerebrum, the cerebellum and the brain stem. The brainstem which includes the medulla, the pons and the midbrain, controls breathing, digestion, heart rate and other autonomic processes, as well as connecting the brain with the spinal cord and the rest of the body. The cerebellum plays an important role in balance, motor control, but is also involved in some cognitive functions such as attention, language, emotional functions (such as regulating fear and pleasure responses) and in the processing of procedural memories. The cerebrum (or forebrain), which makes up 75% of the brain by volume and 85% by weight, is divided by a large groove, known as the longitudinal fissure, into two distinct hemispheres. The left and right hemispheres ("left" and "right" refer to the owner's point of view, not an outside viewer's) are linked by a large bundle of nerve fibers called the corpus callosum, and also by other smaller connections called commissures. Most of the important elements of the cerebrum are split into symmetrical pairs in the left and right hemispheres. Thus, we often speak of the temporal lobes, hippocampi (in the plural), although this website generally follows the convention of speaking of the temporal lobe, hippocampus (in the singular), which should therefore be taken to mean both sides, within both hemispheres. The two hemispheres look similar, but are slightly different in structure and perform different functions. The right hemisphere generally controls the left side of the body, and vice versa, although popular notions that logic and creativity are restricted to the left or right hemispheres are largely simplistic and unfounded. The cerebrum is covered by a sheet of neural tissue known as the cerebral cortex (or neocortex), which envelops other brain organs such as the thalamus (which evolved to help relay information from the brain stem and spinal cord to the cerebral cortex) and the hypothalamus and pituitary gland (which control visceral functions, body temperature and behavioral responses such as feeding, drinking, sexual response, aggression and pleasure). The cerebral cortex itself is only 2 - 4 mm thick, and contains six distinct but interconnected layers. It is intricately grooved and folded into the familiar convoluted pattern of folds, or gyri, allowing a large surface area (typically almost 2 square meters) to fit within the confines of the skull. Consequently, more than two-thirds of the cerebral cortex is buried in the grooves, or sulci. About 90% of all the brain's neurons are located in the cerebral cortex, mainly in the "grey matter", which makes up the surface regions of the cerebral cortex, while the inner "white matter" consists mainly of myelinated axons, over 170,000 km of them. As many as five times that number of glial cells exists to support the active nerve cells. The cerebral cortex plays a key role in memory, attention, perceptual awareness, thought, language and consciousness. It is divided into four main regions or lobes, which cover both hemispheres: the frontal lobe (involved in conscious thought and higher mental functions such as decision-making, particularly in that part of the frontal lobe known as the prefrontal cortex, and plays an important part in processing short-term memories and retaining longer term memories which are not task-based); the parietal lobe (involved in integrating sensory information from the various senses, and in the manipulation of objects in determining spatial sense and navigation); the temporal lobe (involved with the senses of smell and sound, the processing of semantics in both speech and vision, including the processing of complex stimuli like faces and scenes, and plays a key role in the formation of long-term memory); and the occipital lobe (mainly involved with the sense of sight). The medial temporal lobe (the inner part of the temporal lobe, near the divide between the left and right hemispheres) in particular is thought to be involved indeclarative and episodic memory. Deep inside the medial temporal lobe is the region of the brain known as the limbic system, which includes the hippocampus, the amygdala, the cingulate gyrus, the thalamus, the hypothalamus, the epithalamus, the mammillary body and other organs, many of which are of particular relevance to the processing of memory. The hippocampus, for example, is essential for memory function, particularly the transference from short- to long-term memory and control of spatial memory and behavior. The hippocampus is one of the few areas of the brain capable actually growing new neurons, although this ability is impaired by stress-related glucocorticoids. The amygdala also performs a primary role in the processing and memory of emotional reactions and social and sexual behavior, as well as regulating the sense of smell. Another sub-cortical system (inside the cerebral cortex) which is essential to memory function is the basal ganglia system, particularly the striatum (orneostriatum) which is important in the formation and retrieval of procedural memory. The core component of the nervous system in general and the brain in particular, is the neuron or nerve cell, the "brain cells" of popular language. A neuron is an electrically excitable cell that processes and transmits information by electro-chemical signaling. Unlike other cells, neurons never divide, and neither do they die off to be replaced by new ones. By the same token, they usually cannot be replaced after being lost, although there are a few exceptions. The average human brain has about 100 billion neurons (or nerve cells) and many more neuroglia (or glial cells) which serve to support and protect the neurons (although see the end of this page for more information on glial cells). Each neuron may be connected to up to 10,000 other neurons, passing signals to each other via as many as 1,000 trillion synaptic connections, equivalent by some estimates to a computer with a 1 trillion bit per second processor. Estimates of the human brain's memory capacity vary wildly from 1 to 1,000 terabytes (for comparison, the 19 million volumes in the US Library of Congress represents about 10 terabytes of data).

CHAPTER 2

MEMORY ENHANCING
TECHNIQUES

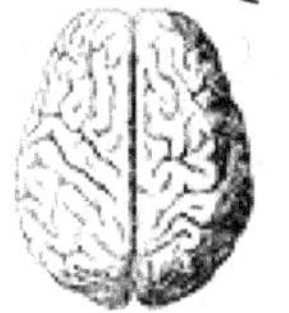

CHAPTER 2.1 – LOCI METHOD

Loci Method, also known under the more popular name of the Mind Palace technique or Memory Palace, got the name from the Latin word Loci, meaning "places". It is a mnemonic device used for the first time in the ancient Rome and Greece, as it is mentioned in some rhetorical treatise such as Cicero's "Rhetorica ad herenium" and Quintilian's "Institutio Oratoria". It is one of the oldest known mnemonic techniques. According to Cicero, the Loci method was developed by the poet Simonides of Ceos. He was the only survivor of a building collapse that happened during a dinner. He was able to identify the crushed bodies by remembering where each guest has been sitting. In that moment he realized that you can remember anything if you associate it with a mental image of a well-known location.

How do you learn it? You can easily remember a place that you are familiar with it, like the home where you grew up or your first school. You can use a mental link between various spots from that place and other unrelated informations. Greeks and Romans orators used Loci as a tool, helping them to give speeches without the aid of notes. Dating back from 500 B.C., Loci Method was the most popular mnemonic system until in the sixteen century, when the phonetic and peg system were invented. If you are a visual type, this method will work with increased efficiency for you.

Now I will teach you how to use it:

1. Take the first book that you can find around you. Open the book at the chapter's page and skim through the names. How good do you think you are at memorizing all the names of every chapter? Think now at a place that you know very well. Could be the part of the town where you grew up as a child.

2. Visualize a series of locations in logical order. Let's say the book has 5 chapters. You leave your flat and walk by the corner shop, fruit market, drugstore and Italian restaurant. You can use other locations if you need them, but in the beginning start by using only 10-20 places or locations.

3. Now link each chapter with one of these places. When you want to remember the names of each chapter, just visualize yourself walking through your town using this mental path. Each name that you associated with a specific location should spring to mind as you mentally make your walk through the town.

The names of the chapters are: The shaving cream experiment, The hot-dog vendor, The ice-cream in the afternoon, Peaches and beaches, The black spot. You will imagine a huge shaving cream spray near the exit door, then the corner shop vendor in the front of his shop cooking hot dogs, then a beautiful girl having an ice-cream as she is going through the fruit market in the afternoon, and she is checking her watch only to see that it is 5 o'clock, then a big promotion at the drugstore for sunscreen protection cream made from peaches, to use at the beach, because you will go in holiday soon, in Malta, and in the end, a waiter with a huge black spot on his nose.

Remember, your mental image needs to be original, unusual and outrageous, to make it easier to remember. You can use Loci to memorize lists, names, key points of a speech or even entire books (the last one in combination with few other memory enhancing techniques). The research behind this method proved it efficient because this it is a form of elaborate rehearsal, and you create a link between new memories and old, already consolidated memories, using familiar places to cue yourself about the new information. Because you already know that place very well, the memories flow effortlessly one into the next one in a fluid move. You can adapt this to remember bigger quantities of information using buildings, areas or even cities or countries (Work places, schools or universities, native town). You can link different informations with different buildings or places, the distance between them is irrelevant (I use a fast speeding train that is taking me from one place to another in a fraction of a second). You can also place more than one piece of information at each location, so if you have 40 items on a list and 8 good locations, you can use each location to place 5 items. Let's say that you have a building with 8 rooms. You can place 5 items in each room, linking each 5 items in a short phrase (see Narrative Chaining technique). A trick to use in order to avoid going through the whole linking process to remember for example item 32, without remembering the previous 31, is to use a distinctive mark at every place that you used. At the fifth place I will have a porcelain blue hand with 5 fingers, at the tenth place I will have a ten pounds note, at the fifteen place I will have a pink electronic clock showing the time 15:00 and the example can go on and on. A very similar strategy can be used to remember the name of 10-15 guests at a party, where all the 15 were introduced to you. This is also a great trick to entertain everyone, if you are aiming at the ideal of a photographic memory.

CHAPTER 2.2 – NARRATIVE CHAINING

This method is based on the creation of a short story or long phrase that contains the information that needs to be remembered. The Narrative Chaining method puts unorganized information into a meaningful context, facilitating the movement of the information from short term memory into the long term memory, as the later one is coded semantically. Using this technique, the retention is greatly improved.

Bowler and Clark experiments, done in 1969, studied two groups of people, needing to learn 12 lists of 12 words, randomly chosen. Using the previously mentioned technique, the trained group memorized 135 words on average (94%), while the control group, without any memory enhancing technique, memorized 20 words on average (14%). The Narrative Chaining method is better than any other mnemonic technique at memorizing lists, items, names or numbers. It can be improved even more if you will use mental imagery, creating a visual connection or interaction between separate items represented in the narrative chain. In the Linda Catering experiment different techniques were used, and this was the best method, superior to Loci, acronyms, keywords or the elaboration method. Known also under the name of Linking Method, based on the linking of the information from a list into a sentence or a story, a form of elaborative rehearsal, this was also the faster in terms of time spent on memorization, hence the most efficient one in learning serial lists. By the use of words and the association to each other, the new words and the others already stored into the long term memory end up creating a stronger connection between them. In 1963, the Young and Gibson experiment started with 12 lists of 12 words each, and after the training group becomes familiar with the technique, after the first four lists, the retention rate was bigger than 99% (93% median) versus the control group (13%).

You only need fifteen minutes of practice in order to improve your skills using the Narrative Chaining, and push the retention rate from 13-14% up to 93-99%. In the case of the experiments mentioned on this chapter, all 12 words were used in one phrase, and the imagery usage will put you close to 100% retention.

Bibliography for in-depth study on Chain Linking:
K.A.Ericsson – Deliberate practice
Ed Cooke – KL7 Deck training
Joshua Foer – Moonlighting with Einstein: The art and the science of remembering anything.

CHAPTER 2.3 – THE PEG WORDS STRATEGY

This method is using the principles of learning and recalling new information by association with familiar facts. You will also need a minimal training in order to learn how to use it proficiently. There are two versions, one using the number-rhyme association and the other using the number-shape association. There are many versions of the PEG Method alphabet, and I will write here one on them. Remember (pun intended), this is the most efficient method for the memorization of a list of less than 10 numbers, in a particular order.

The rhyme list that I used lately is this:
Zero is a hero
One is a bun
Two is a shoe
Three is a tree
Four is a door
Five is a hive
Six – sticks
Seven is heaven
Eight is gate
Nine is wine
Ten is a hen.

How to use this list? Learn the rhyme until you know it by heart, and link each number to the item of the list, and used as it is, or as a side technique in combo with the Narrative Chaining, for phone numbers.

Example:
My phone number is 07769507371, she said.

In your mind you instantly say:
"A League of Legend hero (0) named Jinx, come twice for heaven (77), she got her sticks (6) and she broke a bottle of wine (9). A Hive (5) ship attacks the hero (0), send her back to heaven (7), then a tree (3) grows in the heaven (7) and she is eating a bun (1) under it.
The number is 07769507371.

The second version is using the shape of the numbers as you can see in the following list:
1 – Candle, straw, stick, pencil, leg, finger, light house
2 – Duck, swan, goose, flamingo
3 – Moustache sidebar, camel's hump, worm, snake, ostrich, butterfly, double chin, lips, heart, and cuffs
4 – Sail, flag
5 – Meat hook, wheelchair, cymbal and drum, pulley, seahorse
6 – Cherry, snail house, elephant trunk, pipe, ram's horn, golf club, whistle
7 – Cliff, hammer, boomerang, axe, scythe, gun, giraffe
8 – Snowman, hourglass, spectacles, two plates, two donuts, two buns, two balls, shapely woman, winding key
9 – Balloon, hunting horn, lollipop, tadpole, tennis racket, comma
10 – Road sign and ball, stick and donut, knife and plate.

CHAPTER 2.4 – MAJOR SYSTEM

The Major System (also called the phonetic number system, phonetic mnemonic system, or Herigone's mnemonic system) is a mnemonic technique used to aid in memorizing numbers. The system works by converting numbers into consonant sounds, then into words by adding vowels. The system works on the principle that images can be remembered more easily than numbers. Each numeral is associated with one or more consonants. Vowels and the consonants w, h, and y are ignored. These can be used as "fillers" to make sensible words from the resulting consonant sequences.

A standard mapping is:

Numeral Sounds (IPA)
Commonly associated letters
Mnemonic and remarks

0/s/, /z/   s, soft c, z, x (in xylophone and anxiety)
Zero begins with z (and /z/). Upper case S and Z, as well as lower case s and z, have zero vertical strokes each, as with the numeral 0. The alveolar fricatives /s/ and /z/ form a voiceless and voiced pair.

1/t/, /d/, (/θ/, /ð/)   t, d, (th in thing and this)
Upper case T and D, as well as lower case t and d have one vertical stroke each, as with the numeral 1. The alveolar stops /t/ and /d/ form a voiceless and voiced pair, as do the similar sounding dental fricatives /θ/ and /ð/, though some variant systems may omit the latter pair.

2/n/n   Upper case N and lower case n each have two vertical strokes and two points on the baseline.

3/m/   m Lower case m has three vertical strokes. Both upper case M and lower case m each have three points on the baseline and look like the numeral 3 on its side.

4/r/ r, l (in colonel) Four ends with r (and /r/ in rhotic accents).

5/l/ l   L is the Roman numeral for 50. Among the five digits of one's left hand, the thumb and index fingers also form an L.

6/tʃ/, /dʒ/, /ʃ/, /ʒ/   ch (in cheese and chef), j, soft g, sh, c (in cello and special), cz (in Czech), s (in tissue and vision), sc (in fascist), sch (in schwa and eschew), t (in ration and equation), tsch (in putsch), z (in seizure) Upper case G and lower case g look like the numeral 6 flipped horizontally and rotated 180° respectively. Lower case script j tends to have a lower loop, like the numeral 6. In some serif fonts, upper case CH, SH and ZH each have six serifs. The post alveolar affricates /tʃ/ and /dʒ/ form a voiceless and voiced pair, as do the similar sounding post alveolar fricatives /ʃ/ and /ʒ/.

7/k/, /g/   k, hard c, q, ch (in loch), hard g Both upper case K and lower case k look like two small 7s on their sides. In some fonts, the lower-right part of the upper case G looks like a 7. The velar stops /k/ and /g/ form a voiceless and voiced pair.

8/f/, /v/   f, ph (in phone), v Lower case script f, which tends to have an upper and lower loop, looks like a figure-8. The labiodental fricatives /f/ and /v/ form a voiceless and voiced pair.

9/p/, /b/   p, b, gh (in hiccough) Upper case P and lower case p look like the numeral 9 flipped horizontally. Lower case b looks like the numeral 9 turned 180°. The labial stops /p/ and /b/ form a voiceless and voiced pair.

Unassigned   /h/, /j/, /w/, vowel sounds   h, y, w, a, e, i, o, u, silent letters, c (in packet and chutzpah), d (in judge), j (in Hallelujah and jalapeno), ll (in tortilla), the first p in sapphire, t (in match), one of doubled letters in most contexts   Vowel sounds, semivowels (/j/ and /w/) and /h/ do not correspond to any number. They can appear anywhere in a word without changing its number value.

(2, 27 or 7)   /ŋ/ ng, n before k, hard c, q, hard g or x   Variant systems differ about whether /ŋ/ should encode 2 and classified together with /n/, 7 and classified together with /k/ and /g/ or even 27 (e.g. ring could be 42, 47 or 427). When a /k/ and /g/ is pronounced separately after the /ŋ/, variant systems that chose /ŋ/ to be 27 also disagree if an extra 7 should be written (e.g. finger could be 8274 or 82774, or if /ŋ/ is chosen to be 7, 8774).

The groups of similar sounds and the rules for applying the mappings are almost always fixed, but other hooks and mappings can be used as long as the person using the system can remember them and apply them consistently.

Each numeral maps to a set of similar sounds with similar mouth and tongue positions. The link is phonetic, that is to say, it is the consonant sounds that matter, not the spelling. Therefore, a word like action would encode the number 762 (/k/-/ʃ/-/n/), not 712 (k-t-n). Double letters are disregarded when not pronounced separately, e.g. muddy encodes 31 (/m/-/d/), not 311, but midday encodes 311 (/m/-/d/-/d/) while accept encodes 7091 (/k/-/s/-/p/-/t/) since the ds and cs are pronounced separately. x encodes 70 when pronounced as /ks/ or /gz/ (e.g. in fax and exam) and 76 when pronounced /kʃ/ or /gʒ/ (e.g. in action or luxury); z encodes 10 when pronounced /ts/ (e.g. in pizza). In ghost (701, /g/-/s/-/t/)

and enough (28, /n/-/f/), gh is being encoded by different numerals. Usually, a rhotic accent is assumed, e.g. fear would encode 84 (/f/-/r/) rather than 8 (/f/).

Often the mapping is compact. Hindquarters, for example, translates unambiguously to 2174140 (/n/-/d/-/k/-/r/-/t/-/r/-/z/), which amounts to seven digits encoded by eight letters, and can be easily visualized.

Each numeral maps to a set of similar sounds with similar mouth and tongue positions. For most people it would be easier to remember 3.1415927 (an approximation of the mathematical constant pi) as:

meteor (314, /m/-/t/-/r/)
tail (15, /t/-/l/)
pink (927, /p/-/ŋ/-/k/, and taking /ŋ/ to be 2)
Short term visual memory of imagined scenes allows large numbers of digits to be memorized with ease, though usually only for a short time.

Whilst this is unwieldy at first, with practice it can become a very effective technique. [citation needed] Longer-term memory may require the formulation of more object-related mnemonics with greater logical connection, perhaps forming grammatical sentences that apply to the matter rather than just strings of images.

The system can be employed with phone numbers. One would typically make up multiple words, preferably a sentence, or an ordered sequence of images featuring the owner of the number.

The Major System can be combined with a peg system for remembering lists, and is sometimes used also as a method of generating the pegs. It can also be combined with other memory techniques such as rhyming, substitute words, or the method of loci. Repetition and concentration using the ordinary memory is still required.

An advantage of the major system is that it is possible to use a computer to automatically translate the number into a set of words. One can then pick the best of several alternatives. Such programs include "Numzi", "Rememberg", "Fonbee", the freeware "2Know", and the website "pinfruit".

Some of these example words may belong to more than one word category.

1-digit pegs

0   1   2   3   4   5   6   7   8   9

noun: hose   hat   hen home   arrow   whale   shoe
   cow   hoof   pie

verb: sew   hate   know   aim   row   heal   chew
   hook   view   buy

adjective : easy   hot new   yummy hairy   oily
   itchy   gay heavy   happy

2-digit pegs

00   01   02   03   04   05   06   07   08   09

noun: sauce seed   sun sumo   sierra   soil sewage sky
  sofa   soap

verb: assess   swat   assign assume sorrow sell
  switch soak   save   sob

adjective : sissy sad snowy awesome   sorry   slow
  swishy sicksavvy   sappy

10   11 12 13 14 15 16 17 18 19

noun: daisy   tattoo tuna   dome   diary   tail
  dish   dogdove   tuba

verb: tease   editwiden time   draw   tell teach
  take   defy   type

adjective: dizzy   tight   wooden   tame   dry tall
  whitish thick   deaf   deep

20   21 22 23 24 25 26 27 28 29

noun: nose   net onion   enemy winery nail nacho
  neck   knife   honeybee

verb: ionize unite   nanny name   honor [inhale
  enjoy   knock envy   nab

adjective: noisy   neat   neon   numb   narrow
  annual nudgy naggy naïve   wannabe

30   31 32 33 34 35 36 37 38 39

noun: mouse meadow   moon mummy   emery
mole   match mug   movie map

verb: amuse meet   mine   mime marry mail
mash   mock move   mop

adjective : messy mute   mean   mum   merry male
mushy mucky mauve wimpy

40   41 42 43 44 45 46 47 48 49

noun: rice   road   urine   rum   aurora railway
roach   rag roof   rope

verb: erase   read   ruin   ram rear [a] rule reach
rake   arrive wrap

adjective: rosy   ready   runny haram rare
royal   rich rocky   rough   ripe

50   51 52 53 54 55 56 57 58 59

noun: louse lady   lion lime   lorry   lily leech   leg
lava lip

verb: lose   let align   loom   lure   lull latch   lick
love   help
adjective: lazy elite   alien   lame   leery   loyal
yellowish   lucky   leafy   loopy

60   61 62 63 64 65 66 67 68 69

noun: cheese cheetah   chin   gem   shrew   chili
 cha-cha   chick   chef   jeep
verb: chase   cheat   chain   jam jury   chill
 judge   check   achieve chop
adjective: choosy chatty shiny   sham   cherry
 jolly   Jewish shaky   chief   cheap

70   71 72 73 74 75 76 77 78 79

noun: goose   cat coin   game   crow   clay cage
 cake   cave   cube

verb: kiss quote weaken comb carry   kill coach
 cook   give   copy

adjective : cozy   good   keen   gummy grey   cool
 catchy quick   goofy   agape

80   81 82 83 84 85 86 87 88 89

noun: vase   video   fan ovum   fairy   fool   veggie
 fig fife vibe
verb: fuse   fight   fine fume   fry fly fetch
 fake   viva   fob
adjective : fussy fat funny   foamy   furry   foul
 fishy   foggy   fave   fab

90   91 92 93 94 95 96 97 98 99

noun: boss   bead   pony   puma   berry   bell
 pouch bike   beef   pipe

verb: oppose bite   ban bomb bury   peel   patch
  poke   pave   pop
adjective: busy   bad   bony   balmy pro blue
  bushy back   puffy   baby

A different memory system, the method of loci was taught to schoolchildren for centuries, at least until 1584, "when Puritan reformers declared it unholy for encouraging bizarre and irreverent images." The same objection can be made over the major system, with or without the method of loci. Mental images may be easier to remember if they are insulting, violent, or obscene (see Von Restorff effect). Pierre Hérigone (1580–1643) was a French mathematician and astronomer and devised the earliest version of the major system. The major system was further developed by Stanislaus Mink von Wennsshein 300 years ago. It was later elaborated upon by other users. In 1730, Richard Grey set forth a complicated system that used both consonants and vowels to represent the digits. In 1808 Gregor von Feinaigle introduced the improvement of representing the digits by consonant sounds (but reversed the values of 8 and 9 compared to those listed above). In 1825 French scientist Aimé Paris published the first known version of the major system in its modern form. In 1844 Francis Fauvel Gouraud (1808-1847) delivered a series of lectures introducing his mnemonic system which was based on Aimé Paris' version. The lectures drew some of the largest crowds ever assembled to hear lectures of a "scientific" nature up to that time. This series of lectures was later published as Phreno-Mnemotechny or The Art of Memory in 1845 and his system received wide acclaim. According to Gouraud, Richard Grey indicated that a discussion on Hebrew linguistics in William Beveridge's Institutionum chronotogicarum libri duo, una cum totidem arithmetices chronologicæ libellis (London, 1669) inspired him to create his system of mnemotechniques which later evolved in to the major system. The system described in this article would again be popularized by Harry Lorayne, a bestselling contemporary author on memory. The name "major system" refers to Major Beniowski, who published a version of the system in his book, The Anti-Absurd or Phrenotypic English Pronouncing and Orthographical Dictionary. There is a reasonable historical possibility that the roots of the Major System are entangled with older systems of Shorthand. It is certainly the case that the underlying structure of the Major System has a direct overlap with Gregg shorthand, which was a popular shorthand system in the late 1800s and early 1900s. Phonetic number memorization systems also occur in other parts of the world, such as the Katapayadi system going back to at least the 7th Century in India.

Practice

Memory feats centered on numbers can be performed by experts who have learned a 'vocabulary' of at least 1 image for every 1 and 2 digit number which can be combined to form narratives. To learn a vocabulary of 3 digit numbers is harder because for each extra digit 10 times more images need to be learned, but many mnemonists use a set of 1000 images. Combination of images into a narrative is easier to do rapidly than is forming a coherent, grammatical sentence. This pre-memorisation and practice at forming images reduces the time required to think up a good imaginary object and create a strong memorable impression of it. The best words for this purpose are usually nouns, especially those for distinctive objects which make a strong impression on a variety of senses (e.g. a "Lime" for 53, its taste, its smell, its color and even its texture are distinctive) or which move (like an "arrow" for 4). For basic proficiency a large vocabulary of image words isn't really necessary since, when the table above is reliably learned, it is easy to form your own words ad hoc. Mnemonics often concentrate around learning a complete sequence where all objects in that sequence that come before the one you are trying to recall must be recalled first. For instance, if you were using the mnemonic "Richard of York gave battle in vain" for the colours of the rainbow; (red, orange, yellow, green, blue, indigo and violet) to remember what colours comes after indigo you would have to recall the whole sequence. For a short sequence this may be trivial; for longer lists, it can become complicated and error-prone. A good example would be in recalling what the 53rd element of the periodic table is. It might be possible for some people to construct and then learn a string of 53 or more items which you have substituted for the elements and then to recall them one by one, counting them off as you go, but it would be a great deal easier and less laborious/tedious to directly associate element 53 with, for example, a lime (a suitable mnemonic for 53) recalling some prior imagining of yours regarding a mishap where lime juice gets into one's eye - "eye" sounding like "I", the symbol for Iodine. This allows for random access directly to the item, without the need for recalling any previous items. If you were remembering element 53 in the process of recalling the periodic table you could then recall an image for 54, for instance thinking of a friend called "Laura" (54) in the lotus position looking very Zen-like in order to remind yourself that element 54 is Xenon. This is an example of combining the Major System with the peg system.

CHAPTER 2.5 – DOMINIC SYSTEM

The Dominic system is a mnemonic system used to remember sequences of digits similar to the mnemonic major system. It was invented and used in competition by eight-time World Memory Champion Dominic O'Brien.

The main difference between the Dominic system and the major system is the assignment of sounds and letters to digits. The Dominic system is a letter-based abbreviation system where the letters comprise the initials of someone's name, while the major system is typically used as a phonetic-based consonant system for objects, animals, persons, or even words. The major system would assign the sounds T + L to the number 15, and then find a word that has those sounds as the first two consonants. Mnemonic images like Tolkien, tiles, or toolbox could be assigned under the major system. In the Dominic system, 15 would be the letters A and E, and they would be used as the initials of someone's name—for example, Albert Einstein. Albert Einstein would then be given a characteristic action, such as "writing on a blackboard". Each two-digit number would have an associated person and action. The Dominic system is specifically designed as a person-action system, while the major system can also be used to represent stand-alone objects. Many mnemonists use the major system as a person-action system as well, so the main difference is the way that images are assigned to the numbers.

Like the mnemonic major system, the Dominic system can be combined with a memory palace, thereby creating the Hotel Dominic. Using the Dominic system every pair of digits is first associated with a person. Dominic O'Brien feels that stories and images created using people are easier to remember. This encoding is carried out ahead of time and the people are reused, since it can take quite some time. To perform this encoding, each digit is associated with a letter using the table below. These letters then become the initials of the person representing this number. People will often use quite a loose definition of "initials", using the initial letters of a phrase describing a person, such as "80 = HO = Santa Claus, laughing and holding his belly (HO, HO, HO!)".[2]

Number	1	2	3	4	5	6	7	8	9	0
Mnemonic	A	B	C	D	E	S	G	H	N	O

Encoding pairs of digits as actions

Once each pair of digits has been associated with a person one can then cheaply create a corresponding action for each person. For example, if one had chosen to represent AE as the physicist Albert Einstein one might use a corresponding action of writing on a blackboard.

Usage

Once the mappings of pair of digits are in place a sequence of digits can be converted into a story by first encoding pairs of digits as people or actions and then chaining these people and actions together.

For example, one might remember the number 2739 as follows: First 27 would be encoded BG and then as Bill

Gates, then 39 would be encoded as CN and then Chuck Norris. Using the first two digits as a person and the second two as an action, one creates the image of Bill Gates delivering a roundhouse kick. Similarly 3927 might be converted into the image of Chuck Norris writing software. Longer numbers become stories. The long number 27636339, for example, could be chunked into 2763 6339 and then converted into BGSC SCCN. If the memorizer has also associated Santa Claus delivering presents with SC, then the chunk 2763 would represent Bill Gates delivering presents while 6339 would represent Santa Claus performing a roundhouse kick. The remembered story, therefore, could be that Bill Gates delivered presents and then got roundhouse kicked by Santa Claus.

The Dominic System is typically used along with the method of loci, which allows the easy recall of the images in order by placing them in locations along a mental journey.

Packs of cards

Although the Dominic system is a method for remembering long sequences of numbers, it can also be used to remember other sequences such as the order of a deck of playing cards. This works by establishing some method of systematically converting the objects into numbers. If the nine of clubs is associated with 39 (CN), for instance, then Chuck Norris or a roundhouse kick could be used in a story describing where the nine of clubs is in the deck.

CHAPTER 2.6 ACROSTICS

Acrostic poems have been around for centuries. The earliest record of an acrostic use is in the prophesies of the Eritrean Sibyl, prophetesses who were believed to have predicted the Trojan War and other historical events. The prophesies were written on leaves, and then the leaves were positioned so that the first letter of each leaf created a word.

An acrostic poem was also found at Pompeii during an archaeological excavation. Since the messages in acrostics are usually visible only when it is understood when each line of poetry begins and ends, it is believed that, unlike other poetic forms, acrostic poetry was first written rather than passed down orally. Acrostics have been around so long that they've had their brushes with lasting fame. As an example, one religious Greek acrostic is Iesous Christos, Theou Yios, Soter, which means Jesus Christ, God's Son, Savior. You may know that the emblem of paleo-Christians was the fish. The Greek word for the fish is "ἰχθὺς" (Ichthys). And here is what it stands for if you are one of the first Christians.

ΙΧΘΥΣ

I (I, Iota) : ΙΗΣΟΥΣ (Iêsoûs) « Jesus »
X (KH, Khi) : ΧΡΙΣΤΟΣ (Khristòs) « Christ » ;
Θ (TH, Theta) : ΘΕΟΥ (Theoû) « God » ;
Υ (U, Upsilon) : ΥΙΟΣ (Huiòs) « Son » ;
Σ (S, Sigma) : ΣΩΤΗΡ (Sôtér) « Saver ».

INRI

And on the same theme, the acronym INRI (so often seen on crucifixes), but Latin this time:

I : IESVS : Jesus
N : NAZARENVS : Nazarene
R : REX : King
I : IVDÆORVM : of the Jews

The mental contraption fits that acrostics inspire have attracted famous people in history. Acrostic poems can be found in many different types of literature. There are at least 12 clear examples of acrostics in the Old Testament (mostly in the Psalms). Shakespeare is said to have used acrostics to hide messages from Christopher Marlowe, and Edgar Allen Poe wrote a poem titled A Valentine in which he spelled out the name 'Frances Sargent Osgood'. Same Edgar Allan Poe interwove acrostics into his work. He actually titled one of his poems, "An Acrostic," and the not-so-hidden message spelled out Elizabeth, a female admirer. Some writers would decorate the first letters of each line to stand out, while others, especially Renaissance writers, would use the poems as hidden messages. It is believed that double acrostics were invented during the 18th century. These poems use letters at both the beginning and end of each line to spell out a message. Here is an example of a double acrostic:

Fly by the seat of your pants, nothing planned
Unfettered life, free to travel to any area
New adventures await every step of the way

Lewis Carroll, for example, included an acrostic in his story, "Through the Looking Glass." A poem in the story's final chapter spells out the full name of Carroll's most famous character: Alice Pleasance Liddell, who of is the heroine in "Alice in Wonderland." As you already know, not all acrostics are puzzles, and there are some notable variants within the acrostic form itself. One type is called double acrostic. In a double acrostic, the first and last letter of each line of text results in the same word or phrase. In an alternate version, the last letters spell the same word, but they do so in reverse order, with the mystery word spelled beginning at the end of the last line. Double acrostics are a type of multiple acrostic. But some acrostics of the multiple type go to the next level, such as with William Browne's poem called "Behold, O God." The poem's text has highlighted letters that, when isolated from the other letters, form three independent phrases, for example, "O God, my God, why hast thou forsaken me?". But this particular multiple acrostic takes things even further. As you push the highlighted letters together, they actually form three crosses. So not only does it result in new phrases, but it celebrates Browne's convictions visually, too. It's no wonder that people who love a good mental workout decided to put acrostics into puzzle form. Speaking of which, we'll take a look at the history and popularity of the acrostic puzzle itself in the next section. You already know that the use of the acrostic as wordplay has a long and storied history. The puzzle form of acrostics, however, is a comparatively new invention. No one knows for sure exactly who had the idea of morphing acrostic poetry into puzzles, but the games did appear in printed form in the middle of 19th century. England's Queen Victoria was a known devotee of acrostics and composed her own puzzles, leading some historians to speculate that perhaps she sparked the acrostic puzzle phenomenon. Modern acrostic puzzles are the brainchild of Elizabeth Kingsley, who first unveiled these games in the Saturday Review in March 1934. Those first puzzles were called Double Crostic. As with most acrostic puzzles, the completed grid unveiled a famous quotation. In addition, the first letter of the answers to clues revealed a title and author of a book, poem or other written work. Kingsley's work proved to be so popular that The New York Times hired her to create acrostic puzzles, too. She composed the puzzles for the paper's readers from May 1943 to the end of 1952. Since then, The New York Times has been known for its challenging acrostics, much as it is known for its synapse-shattering crossword puzzles. Masterful acrostic puzzle makers have called The Times home, and surprisingly, since Kingsley's reign ended, only four other people have authored them, including Doris Wortman, Thomas Middleton and most recently, Emily Cox and Henry Rathvon. The puzzles garnered a rabid fan base and have generally appeared in The Times every two weeks for decades now. And when they don't, a lot of people get very upset, as evidenced by the number of comments and calls The Times receives when substitute puzzles appear in place of acrostics.

Like crossword puzzles, Sudoku and other brain games, acrostics have a devoted following of people who love to tweak their gray matter. These days, fans can find their favorite game in a variety of formats. Publishers, like The New York Times, still print book-bound puzzles of all types, including acrostics collections. You'll find these at well-stocked book stores or through online book retailers. Books are great, but the fastest way to jump into acrostic puzzles is online. With a quick search you'll find numerous sites that let you play immediately, such as The New York Times' Web site. As of this writing, there weren't any apps for Android smartphones, but the Apple App store does allow you to download both a free and paid version of the Crostix app. There are also many sites that let you print puzzles with your home printer. Keep in mind that if you do cheat, you won't get the biggest benefits from acrostic puzzles. Some people think that these types of puzzles might keep the brain working at full capacity or improve word fluency, which helps you remember and pull words from the speech and language areas of your brain. A few experts in an article published in Time Magazine even believe that regularly challenging your brain might help stave off the onset of diseases such as Alzheimer's. Whether puzzles have that kind of power is still up for debate. More certain is the idea that cheating the puzzle is actually cheating any benefit your mind might receive from overcoming those mental obstacles.

CHAPTER 2.7 ACRONYMS

As you can see, acronyms are no recent invention. As for what was the first one, this is probably lost forever. Acronyms didn't become a common method of word formation in English until World War II. The word acronym itself wasn't coined until 1943. The lack of a need for such a word suggests the degree to which acronyms previously were not a part of daily life. Their use accelerated with the U.S. space program and the Cold War, and by the time a "Dictionary of Acronyms, Initialisms and Abbreviations" was published in 1960 it had 12,000 entries.

So acronyms in English are on the whole a 20th century phenomenon. Among those with pre-1900 origins are A.D. and B.C. (both Latin) and P.D.Q. (1870s). The word OK (c.1839) is another rare exception (if the most accepted theory of its origins is the right one), as is n.g. for "no good" (1838). And note how these initialisms, even after more than 170 years, are still "felt" as abbreviations, pronounced as distinct letters, and require no elaborate Internet stories. Other mentions come from the OED dating from 1895: SCOTUS (Supreme Court of the United States), POTUS (President of the United States), from the Phillips Code used "for the rapid transmission of press reports by telegraph", from 1895 and perhaps 1879.

As you might expect, the use of acronyms themselves long predate the coinage of the term. For example, initialisms were used in Rome before the Christian era. For example, the official name for the Roman Empire, and the Republic before it, was abbreviated as SPQR (Senatus Populusque Romanus). Acronyms are very common on Roman coins where writing space is limited: SC: Senatus

Consulto. PM: Pontifex Maximus, SPQR: Senatus PopulusQue Romanus. PF Pius et Felix.

82

Consulto. PM: Pontifex Maximus, SPQR: Senatus PopulusQue Romanus. PF Pius et Felix.

CHAPTER 2.8 – BONUS CHAPTER
HOW TO MEMORIZE WHOLE BOOKS

This is a method developed by me when I was studying in University. I used my dominant sense (which is seeing, and the secondary dominant one which is the kinesthetic one). You can adapt it to yourself if your dominant sense is other than visual or tactile (if you are an auditory person you can read loudly when you are writing for example or read loudly when you finish a step).

I have a whole book, let's say it is a biology one. I will divide in chapters and subchapter. Then I will take the subchapters one by one and I will do a resume of that specific subchapter. Example: Cardiovascular system – chapter, Heart – subchapter. Then I will do a resume of the resume. I will repeat this step as long as is needed until I resumed the whole subchapter as a phrase. Then I will choose one word to define that phrase. At the end, I will use all the subchapter words to make one phrase for the whole chapter. Then I will use one word for the Chapter. Let's say we have 12 chapters, then we can use the Narrative Chaining technique primary to make a phrase for the book. Then I choose a word for the book phrase. I call this the implosion phase – resulting in the whole book compressed in one word.

When you recall the information, you can do it in reverse. The "book word" becomes a phrase using the list of "chapter words". You can also add an extra safety layer, using Loci method to remember the words in the familiar setting. Then you unfold one layer after another. If you need subchapter 2 from the 4th chapter, then you go the word for the 4th chapter, and expand this into that chapter phrase. Then you go to the word for the subchapter 2, and expand gradually, first to the phrase, then to the last resume, unfolding everything from smaller resume to bigger resume, until you reach the final layer, the word-by-word memory of the book. This memory should be a photographic image of every page.

This way you can access a specific page or subchapter, at any time, during the unfolding phase.

And with this our journey ended in here, but not necessarily. You can still find me on my blog studying the intelligence specter, genius and learning disabilities altogether.

My address is: awakethegeniuswithin.blogspot.com .

ABOUT THE AUTHOR

George Mihalache had studied the brain and its capabilities from early age, spending decades researching about the geniality as a condition and about different ways to improve it. With a medical background, and more than 10 years of work related to autism and learning disabilities, he observed both ends of the intelligence spectrum, in order to come to a coherent approach. As for myself, I always enjoyed to read more about our capabilities on his blog https://awakethegeniuswithin.blogspot.com .I hope you will too.

NEVER FORGET

www.ingramcontent.com/pod-product-compliance
Lightning Source LLC
Chambersburg PA
CBHW061503250726

48657CB00005B/1705